No one is listening in

No one is watching y
your thoughts.

This is a safe place, where there is no shame or anxiety
and there's no need to hide anymore.

Honestly I made this journal for myself.
I always felt like some journals were afraid to go
deeper and explore the entire being.
I wanted to explore these journal prompts in detail
allowing myself to finally have a honest conversation
with myself by myself. There are times I want to doodle in
the journal and other times write, so I split the pages.

My hope is that at the end of 90 days, we'll have a better
understanding of what we want AND need
to achieve our dreams and our life's mission.

You're now free to explore, draw, imagine and create.

If this journal has added value to your life, please
let others know where they can get it.

Thank you.

Where Do You Want To Be One Year From Today?

See the End from the Beginning

WHERE DO YOU WANT TO BE ONE YEAR FROM TODAY?

SEE THE END FROM THE BEGINNING

Health At Every Size

WE ALL HAVE THE SAME BODY PARTS JUST ORGANIZED DIFFERENTLY. YOU'RE BEAUTIFUL. BUT ONE IMPORTANT QUESTION WE HAVE TO ASK OURSELVES IS THIS: DOES MY CURRENT BODY ALLOW ME TO DO WHAT I WANT IN LIFE?

I'M GRATEFUL THAT MY BODY:

_____

_____

_____

_____

_____

WHEN DO I FEEL BEST IN MY BODY?:

_____

_____

_____

_____

_____

IMAGINE THAT YOUR BODY COULD SPEAK TO YOU
WHAT WOULD IT TELL YOU IT NEEDS?:

_____

_____

_____

_____

Health At Every Size

We all have the same body parts just organized differently. You're Beautiful. But one important question we have to ask ourselves is this: Does my current body allow me to do what I want in life?

I'm grateful that my body:

When do I feel best in my body?:

Imagine that your body could speak to you
What would it tell you it needs?:

A Walk In The Park........Jurassic park

Describe your relationship with money

_____

_____

_____

_____

_____

_____

_____

_____

_____

_____

_____

_____

_____

_____

_____

_____

_____

A Walk In The Park........Jurassic park

Describe your relationship with money

WHAT MAKES YOU FEEL LOVED?

NATURE? PETS? CUDDLING? RESPECT?

WHAT MAKES YOU FEEL LOVED?

NATURE? PETS? CUDDLING? RESPECT?

HAPPINESS AUDIT

"HAPPINESS IS NOT SOMETHING YOU POSTPONE FOR
THE FUTURE; IT'S SOMETHING YOU DESIGN FOR THE PRESENT"

TIMES YOU WERE HAPPIEST	TIMES YOU WERE SADDEST

HAPPINESS AUDIT

"HAPPINESS IS NOT SOMETHING YOU POSTPONE FOR
THE FUTURE; IT'S SOMETHING YOU DESIGN FOR THE PRESENT"

TIMES YOU WERE HAPPIEST	TIMES YOU WERE SADDEST

TEARS MAY FALL HERE

JUST LAUGH.

WRITE ABOUT THE LAST TIME YOU LAUGHED REALLY HARD.
WHAT WAS SO FUNNY?

_____

_____

_____

_____

_____

_____

_____

_____

_____

_____

_____

_____

_____

_____

_____

_____

JUST LAUGH.

Write about the last time you laughed really hard. What was so funny?

HEY BOO...

WRITE A LETTER TO MONEY, AS IF THEY WERE A PERSON,
TELLING HIM/HER WHAT KIND OF RELATIONSHIP YOU
WOULD LIKE TO HAVE WITH THEM.

HEY BOO...

WRITE A LETTER TO MONEY, AS IF THEY WERE A PERSON, TELLING HIM/HER WHAT KIND OF RELATIONSHIP YOU WOULD LIKE TO HAVE WITH THEM.

BEFORE I WOULD...

IN THE PAST, WHEN YOU HAD AN ARGUMENT WITH
SOMEONE YOU LOVED, HOW DID YOU FEEL AND BEHAVE?
IS THERE ANYTHING ABOUT THAT BEHAVIOR THAT YOU
WOULD LIKE TO CHANGE FOR THE FUTURE?

BEFORE I WOULD...

In the past, when you had an argument with someone you loved, how did you feel and behave? Is there anything about that behavior that you would like to change for the future?

ENERGY AUDIT

MAKE A LIST OF WHAT GIVES YOU ENERGY AND WHAT
DRAINS YOUR ENERGY. AND THEN FIND WAYS TO
DO MORE OF WHAT GIVES YOU ENERGY.

GIVES ENERGY	DRAINS ENERGY

ENERGY AUDIT

MAKE A LIST OF WHAT GIVES YOU ENERGY AND WHAT
DRAINS YOUR ENERGY. AND THEN FIND WAYS TO
DO MORE OF WHAT GIVES YOU ENERGY.

GIVES ENERGY	DRAINS ENERGY

I USED TO HAVE A 10 PACK.

TALK ABOUT THE TIME THAT YOU FELT YOU WERE THE MOST IN SHAPE IN YOUR ENTIRE LIFE. WHAT THINGS WERE YOU ABLE TO DO THAT YOU AREN'T ABLE TO DO NOW? HOW CAN YOU GET BACK TO THIS? OR EVEN A LITTLE BIT CLOSER?

I USED TO HAVE A 10 PACK.

Talk about the time that you felt you were the most in shape in your entire life. What things were you able to do that you aren't able to do now? How can you get back to this? or even a little bit closer?

EXTRA GUACAMOLE PLEASE.

IF YOU RECEIVED $500,000 IN CASH, BUT HAD TO SPEND
IT WITHIN THE NEXT 24 HOURS, HOW WOULD YOU SPEND
IT? BE VERY SPECIFIC, EVEN DOWN TO THE LAST DOLLAR.

EXTRA GUACAMOLE PLEASE.

IF YOU RECEIVED $500,000 IN CASH, BUT HAD TO SPEND IT WITHIN THE NEXT 24 HOURS, HOW WOULD YOU SPEND IT? BE VERY SPECIFIC, EVEN DOWN TO THE LAST DOLLAR.

LOVE IS IN THE AIR... OR IS THAT BACON?

WHAT DO YOU DO WHEN YOU'RE ANGRY (OR DISAPPOINTED) WITH SOMEONE YOU LOVE? DO YOU FEEL GOOD ABOUT YOUR HABITS FOR HANDLING ANGER WITH THE PEOPLE YOU LOVE? WHY OR WHY NOT?

LOVE IS IN THE AIR...
OR IS THAT BACON?

WHAT DO YOU DO WHEN YOU'RE ANGRY (OR DISAPPOINTED) WITH SOMEONE YOU LOVE? DO YOU FEEL GOOD ABOUT YOUR HABITS FOR HANDLING ANGER WITH THE PEOPLE YOU LOVE? WHY OR WHY NOT?

DISCONNECT

WHAT WAS THE MOST PEACEFUL TIME IN YOUR LIFE? WHAT PLACE OR DESTINATION BRINGS THE MOST PEACE? HOW CAN YOU DESIGN A PLACE OF PEACE FOR YOURSELF? SOME PLACE YOU COULD GO EVERY DAY TO TAKE A FEW MINUTES TO YOURSELF.

DISCONNECT

WHAT WAS THE MOST PEACEFUL TIME IN YOUR LIFE? WHAT PLACE OR DESTINATION BRINGS THE MOST PEACE? HOW CAN YOU DESIGN A PLACE OF PEACE FOR YOURSELF? SOME PLACE YOU COULD GO EVERY DAY TO TAKE A FEW MINUTES TO YOURSELF.

LEG DAY? UGH..

WHAT ARE SOME WAYS TO MAKE EXERCISE EVEN MORE FUN?

LEG DAY? UGH..

WHAT ARE SOME WAYS TO MAKE EXERCISE EVEN MORE FUN?

YOLO

IF YOU WEREN'T AFRAID OF FAILING
WHAT WOULD YOU TRY?

_____

_____

_____

_____

_____

_____

_____

_____

_____

_____

_____

_____

_____

_____

_____

_____

YOLO

If you weren't afraid of failing what would you try?

FIRST KNOW THYSELF.

WHAT ARE YOUR 3 MOST MEMORABLE SEXUAL EXPERIENCES? AND WHY?

FIRST KNOW THYSELF.

WHAT ARE YOUR 3 MOST MEMORABLE SEXUAL EXPERIENCES? AND WHY?

HONOR WHERE YOU ARE

WE CAN'T JUST ZIP TO WHERE WE WANT TO BE.
WE GOTTA TRAVEL THERE. AM I TRULY ENJOYING
THE CHAPTER OF MY LIFE THAT I'M IN RIGHT NOW?
WHAT'S KEEPING ME FROM ENJOYING WHERE I AM?

HONOR WHERE YOU ARE

We can't just zip to where we want to be.
We gotta travel there. Am I truly enjoying
the chapter of my life that I'm in right now?
What's keeping me from enjoying where I am?

YOUR PEE IS TALKING

HOW MUCH WATER DO YOU DRINK A DAY? WHAT ARE SOME THINGS YOU CAN DO TO MAKE DRINKING WATER A HABIT?

YOUR PEE IS TALKING

HOW MUCH WATER DO YOU DRINK A
DAY? WHAT ARE SOME THINGS YOU CAN
DO TO MAKE DRINKING WATER A HABIT?

IN THE BEGINNING...

WHAT IS YOUR FIRST MEMORIES ABOUT MONEY?

IN THE BEGINNING...

WHAT IS YOUR FIRST MEMORIES ABOUT MONEY?

MY BED IS MY BEST FRIEND

HOW SATISFIED ARE YOU WITH YOUR SOCIAL LIFE? HOW CAN YOU MAKE IT BETTER?

_____

_____

_____

_____

_____

_____

_____

_____

_____

_____

_____

_____

_____

_____

_____

_____

_____

_____

MY BED IS MY BEST FRIEND

HOW SATISFIED ARE YOU WITH YOUR SOCIAL LIFE? HOW CAN YOU MAKE IT BETTER?

HAPPY PLACE

DESCRIBE SOME OF YOUR HAPPIEST MOMENTS IN YOUR LIFE

HAPPY PLACE

DESCRIBE SOME OF YOUR HAPPIEST MOMENTS IN YOUR LIFE

JUST MOVE

WHAT DOES IT MEAN TO HAVE AN ACTIVE LIFESTYLE? AND HOW CAN YOU BE MORE ACTIVE THORUGOUT THE WEEK?

JUST MOVE

WHAT DOES IT MEAN TO HAVE AN ACTIVE LIFESTYLE? AND HOW CAN YOU BE MORE ACTIVE THORUGOUT THE WEEK?

WE GOT PLACES TO GO

WHAT IS YOUR 1-YEAR FINANCIAL GOAL?
WHAT IS YOUR 5-YEAR FINANCIAL GOAL?
WHAT IS YOUR 10-YEAR FINANCIAL GOAL?

WE GOT PLACES TO GO

WHAT IS YOUR 1-YEAR FINANCIAL GOAL?
WHAT IS YOUR 5-YEAR FINANCIAL GOAL?
WHAT IS YOUR 10-YEAR FINANCIAL GOAL?

I WASN'T READY

DESCRIBE A SEXUAL FANTASY YOU HAVE.

I wasn't ready

Describe a sexual fantasy you have.

LOL, BUT LIKE FOR REAL.

WRITE ABOUT THE LAST FEW TIMES YOU LAUGHED REALLY
HARD. WHAT WAS SO FUNNY? HOW CAN YOU LAUGH MORE?

LOL, BUT LIKE FOR REAL.

WRITE ABOUT THE LAST FEW TIMES YOU LAUGHED REALLY HARD. WHAT WAS SO FUNNY? HOW CAN YOU LAUGH MORE?

I DON'T HAVE ANY BAD HABITS
I AM GOOD AT ALL OF THEM

NAME THREE BAD HABITS YOU WOULD LIKE TO CHANGE. WHY DO YOU WANT TO CHANGE THESE HABITS?

I don't have any bad habits
I am good at all of them

CORRECTION, "WE" WON

IF YOU RECEIVED $500,000 DOLLARS IN CASH BUT HAD TO SPEND IT WITHIN THE NEXT 24 HOURS, HOW WOULD YOU SPEND IT?

CORRECTION, "WE" WON

IF YOU RECEIVED $500,000 DOLLARS IN CASH BUT HAD TO SPEND IT WITHIN THE NEXT 24 HOURS, HOW WOULD YOU SPEND IT?

MORE NAPS PLEASE

WRITE A LETTER TO YOUR OLDER SELF, 20 YEARS FROM NOW. WHAT DOES LIFE LOOK LIKE NOW?

MORE NAPS PLEASE

WRITE A LETTER TO YOUR OLDER SELF, 20 YEARS
FROM NOW. WHAT DOES LIFE LOOK LIKE NOW?

PRESIDENT OF THE UNIVERSE

WHAT WAS YOUR CHILDHOOD DREAM? WHAT DID YOU WANT TO BE WHEN YOU WERE A KID? WHAT HAPPENED TO THAT DREAM?

PRESIDENT OF THE UNIVERSE

WHAT WAS YOUR CHILDHOOD DREAM?
WHAT DID YOU WANT TO BE WHEN YOU WERE
A KID? WHAT HAPPENED TO THAT DREAM?

COMFORT FOODS

WHAT ARE SOME OF YOUR FAVORITE FOODS? WHY THOUGH?

_____

_____

_____

_____

_____

_____

_____

_____

_____

_____

_____

_____

_____

_____

_____

_____

_____

DAY 30 (HEALTH)

COMFORT FOODS

WHAT ARE SOME OF YOUR FAVORITE FOODS? WHY THOUGH?

I NEED A HUGE AMOUNT OF MONEY

WHAT'S SOME OF THE BEST ADVICE YOU HAVE EVER RECEIVED ON FINANCES? WHAT'S SOME OF THE WORST ADVICE?

_____

_____

_____

_____

_____

_____

_____

_____

_____

_____

_____

_____

_____

_____

_____

_____

_____

_____

_____

_____

_____

DAY 31 (WEALTH)

I NEED A HUG_{E AMOUNT OF MONEY}

WHAT'S SOME OF THE BEST ADVICE YOU HAVE EVER
RECEIVED ON FINANCES? WHAT'S SOME OF THE WORST ADVICE?

I WANT TO
MAKE ME PROUD

WHAT WOULD YOUR YOUNGER SELF
BE MOST PROUD OF YOU FOR?

I WANT TO
MAKE ME PROUD

WHAT WOULD YOUR YOUNGER SELF
BE MOST PROUD OF YOU FOR?

PAIN TO VICTORY

WHAT ARE 3 THINGS THAT HAVE HAPPENED TO YOU WHICH WERE DIFFICULT, BUT YOU ARE NOW GRATEFUL FOR THE EXPERIENCE?

PAIN TO VICTORY

WHAT ARE 3 THINGS THAT HAVE HAPPENED
TO YOU WHICH WERE DIFFICULT, BUT YOU
ARE NOW GRATEFUL FOR THE EXPERIENCE?

HEALING STARTS WITHIN

WHEN I'M IN PAIN — PHYSICAL OR EMOTIONAL THE KINDEST THING I CAN DO FOR MYSELF IS:

HEALING STARTS WITHIN

WHEN I'M IN PAIN — PHYSICAL OR EMOTIONAL
THE KINDEST THING I CAN DO FOR MYSELF IS:

SET FOR LIFE

IF YOU DIDN'T HAVE TO WORRY ABOUT MONEY OR PEOPLE'S OPINIONS, WHAT WOULD YOU DO WITH YOUR LIFE?

SET FOR LIFE

IF YOU DIDN'T HAVE TO WORRY ABOUT MONEY OR PEOPLE'S OPINIONS, WHAT WOULD YOU DO WITH YOUR LIFE?

O YEA

IF YOU COULD HAVE THE PERFECT SEX
LIFE RIGHT NOW, WHAT WOULD THAT LOOK LIKE?

O YEA

IF YOU COULD HAVE THE PERFECT SEX
LIFE RIGHT NOW, WHAT WOULD THAT LOOK LIKE?

PEOPLE I WANT TO PUNCH IN THE FACE:

_____

_____

_____

_____

_____

_____

_____

_____

_____

_____

_____

_____

_____

_____

_____

_____

_____

...

PEOPLE I WANT TO PUNCH IN THE FACE:

"I NEED A NAP"

IF MY BODY COULD TALK, IT WOULD SAY...

"I NEED A NAP"

IF MY BODY COULD TALK, IT WOULD SAY…

"WEALTH IS THE PRODUCT OF A MAN'S ABILITY TO THINK"

WHAT IN YOUR OPINION, IS A "GOOD" AMOUNT OF MONEY TO EARN? WHY? IF YOU'RE NOT MAKING THAT AMOUNT, WHAT CAN YOU DO TO CHANGE THAT?

"WEALTH IS THE PRODUCT OF A MAN'S ABILITY TO THINK"

WHAT IN YOUR OPINION, IS A "GOOD" AMOUNT OF MONEY TO EARN? WHY? IF YOU'RE NOT MAKING THAT AMOUNT, WHAT CAN YOU DO TO CHANGE THAT?

"MY BIRTH CONTROL NOW IS JUST TO LEAVE THE LIGHTS ON"

WHAT'S SOME OF THE BEST ADVICE YOU HAVE EVER RECIEVED ON LOVE? WHATS SOME OF THE WORST ADVICE?

_____

_____

_____

_____

_____

_____

_____

_____

_____

_____

_____

_____

_____

_____

_____

_____

_____

DAY 40 (LOVE)

"MY BIRTH CONTROL NOW IS JUST TO LEAVE THE LIGHTS ON"

WHAT'S SOME OF THE BEST ADVICE YOU HAVE EVER RECIEVED ON LOVE? WHATS SOME OF THE WORST ADVICE?

"TO THINE OWN SELF BE TRUE"

WHAT IS A BOOK YOU WISH SOMEONE WOULD WRITE?

MAYBE YOU SHOULD WRITE THAT BOOK.

"TO THINE OWN SELF BE TRUE"

WHAT IS A BOOK YOU WISH SOMEONE WOULD WRITE?

MAYBE YOU SHOULD WRITE THAT BOOK.

SORRY FOR WHAT I SAID
WHEN I WAS HANGRY

WHAT ARE FIVE WAYS YOU COULD IMPROVE
YOUR OVERALL DIET?

SORRY FOR WHAT I SAID WHEN I WAS HANGRY

WHAT ARE FIVE WAYS YOU COULD IMPROVE YOUR OVERALL DIET?

CHOOSE WISELY

IT'S BEEN SAID THAT WE ARE THE SUM AVERAGE OF THE
PEOPLE WE SPEND THE MOST TIME WITH? WRITE DOWN
THE 5 PEOPLE YOU INTERACT WITH THE MOST

CHOOSE WISELY

IT'S BEEN SAID THAT WE ARE THE SUM AVERAGE OF THE
PEOPLE WE SPEND THE MOST TIME WITH? WRITE DOWN
THE 5 PEOPLE YOU INTERACT WITH THE MOST

BESIDES CHOCOLATE YOU'RE MY FAVORITE

WHAT IS THE MOST ROMANTIC OR SEXIEST THING SOMEONE HAS EVER DONE FOR YOU?

BESIDES CHOCOLATE YOU'RE MY FAVORITE

WHAT IS THE MOST ROMANTIC OR SEXIEST THING SOMEONE HAS EVER DONE FOR YOU?

MORE & MORE

OTHER THAN TIME OR MONEY, WHAT I WANT MORE IS:

MORE & MORE

OTHER THAN TIME OR MONEY, WHAT I WANT MORE IS:

WHERE IS THIS KITCHEN THAT EVERYONE SAYS MAKES ABS?

WHO IS SOMEONE THAT INSPIRES YOU WITH THEIR HEALTH AND FITNESS & WHY?

_____

_____

_____

_____

_____

_____

_____

_____

_____

_____

_____

_____

_____

_____

_____

_____

_____

_____

WHERE IS THIS KITCHEN THAT EVERYONE SAYS MAKES ABS?

WHO IS SOMEONE THAT INSPIRES YOU WITH THEIR HEALTH AND FITNESS & WHY?

MY FAVORITE MEMORY IS NOT PAYING BILLS

WHAT DID YOU BUY WITH YOUR MONEY WHEN YOU WERE A KID?

MY FAVORITE MEMORY IS NOT PAYING BILLS

WHAT DID YOU BUY WITH YOUR MONEY WHEN YOU WERE A KID?

YOU DON'T HAVE TO LIKE ME
I LIKE ME
WHAT IS THE MOST LOVING THING YOU'VE EVER DONE FOR YOURSELF?

_____

_____

_____

_____

_____

_____

_____

_____

_____

_____

_____

_____

_____

_____

_____

_____

_____

_____

YOU DON'T HAVE TO LIKE ME
I LIKE ME

WHAT IS THE MOST LOVING THING YOU'VE EVER DONE FOR YOURSELF?

I NEED A 6 MONTH VACATION TWICE A YEAR

WHAT HAS BEEN YOUR BEST TRIP SO FAR?

I NEED A 6 MONTH VACATION TWICE A YEAR

WHAT HAS BEEN YOUR BEST TRIP SO FAR?

NAMASTE IN BED

WHAT SPEAKS TO YOU ON AN SPIRITUAL LEVEL?
(NATURE, POETRY, A QUOTE, MUSIC ECT.) WRITE ABOUT IT.

NAMASTE IN BED

WHAT SPEAKS TO YOU ON AN SPIRITUAL LEVEL?
(NATURE, POETRY, A QUOTE, MUSIC ECT.) WRITE ABOUT IT.

ONE DAY OR DAY ONE

WHAT INVESTMENT ARE YOU WILLING TO MAKE TO GET OR CREATE YOUR DREAM JOB?

ONE DAY OR DAY ONE

WHAT INVESTMENT ARE YOU WILLING TO MAKE TO GET OR CREATE YOUR DREAM JOB?

SOBER SEX MEANS IT'S SERIOUS

How has your views of sex changed over time?

_____

_____

_____

_____

_____

_____

_____

_____

_____

_____

_____

_____

_____

_____

_____

_____

SOBER SEX MEANS IT'S SERIOUS

HOW HAS YOUR VIEWS OF SEX CHANGED OVER TIME?

COLORS ARE NATURES SMILE

WHAT COLORS BRING YOU JOY? WHAT SOUND(S) BRINGS YOU JOY? WHAT SCENT(S) BRING YOU JOY?

DAY 54 (HAPPINESS)

COLORS ARE NATURES SMILE

WHAT COLORS BRING YOU JOY? WHAT SOUND(S)
BRINGS YOU JOY? WHAT SCENT(S) BRING YOU JOY?

YOGA IS JUST SLOW KARATE

CREATE A FUN GAME THAT INVOLVES (SAFELY!) RUNNING, JUMPING, SKIPPING, AND DANCING

YOGA IS JUST SLOW KARATE

CREATE A FUN GAME THAT INVOLVES (SAFELY!) RUNNING, JUMPING, SKIPPING, AND DANCING

SOMETIMES ALL YOU NEED IS A BILLION DOLLARS

WHO IS SOMEONE THAT INSPIRES YOU FINANCIALLY AND WHY?

SOMETIMES ALL YOU NEED
IS A BILLION DOLLARS

WHO IS SOMEONE THAT INSPIRES
YOU FINANCIALLY AND WHY?

BEAUTY IS IN THE EYE OF THE BEER HOLDER

WHAT'S THE SEXIEST OR KINKIEST GIFT YOU'VE EVER GIVEN AND RECEIVED?

BEAUTY IS IN THE EYE
OF THE BEER HOLDER

WHAT'S THE SEXIEST OR KINKIEST GIFT YOU'VE EVER GIVEN AND RECEIVED?

CAN WE SKIP TO THE PART OF MY LIFE WHERE I TRAVEL THE WORLD

DESCRIBE YOUR DREAM VACATION

_____

_____

_____

_____

_____

_____

_____

_____

_____

_____

_____

_____

_____

_____

_____

_____

CAN WE SKIP TO THE PART OF MY LIFE WHERE I TRAVEL THE WORLD

DESCRIBE YOUR DREAM VACATION

PEOPLE CRY NOT BECAUSE THEY'RE WEAK. BUT BECAUSE THEY'VE BEEN STRONG FOR TOO LONG

WRITE ABOUT THE LAST TIME YOU CRIED WHAT CAUSED YOU TO CRY?

PEOPLE CRY NOT BECAUSE THEY'RE WEAK. BUT BECAUSE THEY'VE BEEN STRONG FOR TOO LONG

WRITE ABOUT THE LAST TIME YOU CRIED WHAT CAUSED YOU TO CRY?

TIME IS PRECIOUS
WASTE IT WISELY

HOW DO YOU DEFINE "SUCCESS"? WHAT WILL IT LOOK LIKE ONCE YOU ACHIEVE IT

_____

_____

_____

_____

_____

_____

_____

_____

_____

_____

_____

_____

_____

_____

_____

_____

TIME IS PRECIOUS
WASTE IT WISELY

HOW DO YOU DEFINE "SUCCESS"? WHAT WILL IT LOOK LIKE ONCE YOU ACHIEVE IT

I LOVE MYSELF
LET ME TELL YOU WHY

NAME A THING THAT YOU LOVE ABOUT YOUR BODY
AND THEN A THING YOU LOVE ABOUT YOUR PERSONALITY.

I LOVE MYSELF
LET ME TELL YOU WHY

NAME A THING THAT YOU LOVE ABOUT YOUR BODY
AND THEN A THING YOU LOVE ABOUT YOUR PERSONALITY.

WHY NOT?

NAME 3 SKILLS YOU'D LOVE TO LEARN WITHIN THE NEXT 3 YEARS. 1ST YEAR; SKILL A. 2ND YEAR; SKILL B. 3RD YEAR; SKILL C

WHY NOT?

NAME 3 SKILLS YOU'D LOVE TO LEARN WITHIN THE NEXT 3 YEARS. 1ST YEAR; SKILL A. 2ND YEAR; SKILL B. 3RD YEAR; SKILL C

EVERYTHING.
WHAT IS YOUR FAVORITE COMFORT FOOD?

EVERYTHING.
WHAT IS YOUR FAVORITE COMFORT FOOD?

WE WERE BORN TO REAL NOT TO BE PERFECT

WHAT'S THE MOST MONEY YOU'VE EVER SPENT ON SOMETHING? GIVE A FEW EXAMPLES

_____

_____

_____

_____

_____

_____

_____

_____

_____

_____

_____

_____

_____

_____

_____

_____

_____

_____

WE WERE BORN TO REAL NOT TO BE PERFECT

WHAT'S THE MOST MONEY YOU'VE EVER SPENT ON SOMETHING? GIVE A FEW EXAMPLES

LET'S MAKE SOME
NEW MISTAKES

WRITE A LETTER TO YOUR PAST SELF. A LETTER
FORGIVING YOURSELF FOR THE MISTAKES YOU'VE MADE

LET'S MAKE SOME
NEW MISTAKES

WRITE A LETTER TO YOUR PAST SELF. A LETTER
FORGIVING YOURSELF FOR THE MISTAKES YOU'VE MADE

I WISH A MF WOULD

WHAT WOULD YOU DO IF YOU WERE GRANTED THREE WISHES?

_____

_____

_____

_____

_____

_____

_____

_____

_____

_____

_____

_____

_____

_____

_____

_____

_____

_____

_____

_____

_____

DAY 66 (HAPPINESS)

I WISH A MF WOULD

WHAT WOULD YOU DO IF YOU WERE GRANTED THREE WISHES?

HOW DO I LIKE MY EGGS?
......IN A CAKE.

THE KITCHEN IS THE ONE AREA WE ALL NEED TO SLOW DOWN IN
HOW CAN YOU PREPARE AND EAT HEALTHIER MEALS?

HOW DO I LIKE MY EGGS?
......IN A CAKE.

THE KITCHEN IS THE ONE AREA WE ALL NEED TO SLOW DOWN IN HOW CAN YOU PREPARE AND EAT HEALTHIER MEALS?

DON'T GROW UP, ISSA TRAP.

CLOSE YOUR EYES AND TRAVEL TO THE FUTURE. FEEL
THE FEELING OF HAVING YOUR FINANCIAL DESIRES
ALREADY FULFILLED. HOW DOES THAT MAKE YOU FEEL?

DON'T GROW UP, ISSA TRAP.

CLOSE YOUR EYES AND TRAVEL TO THE FUTURE. FEEL
THE FEELING OF HAVING YOUR FINANCIAL DESIRES
ALREADY FULFILLED. HOW DOES THAT MAKE YOU FEEL?

TACOS.

WHAT IS YOUR PRIMARY LOVE LANGUAGE?
WORDS OF AFFIRMATION, PHYSICAL TOUCH,
QUALITY TIME, ACTS OF SERVICE OR GIFTS

TACOS.

WHAT IS YOUR PRIMARY LOVE LANGUAGE?
WORDS OF AFFIRMATION, PHYSICAL TOUCH,
QUALITY TIME, ACTS OF SERVICE OR GIFTS

WHAAA $\longrightarrow$

"A LOT OF OUR PROBLEMS COULD BE SOLVED IF WE WOULD JUST SIT QUIETLY IN A ROOM AND THINK DEEPLY"

PROBLEM:

_____

_____

_____

SOLUTION:

1. _____

2. _____

3. _____

4. _____

5. _____

6. _____

7. _____

8. _____

9. _____

10. _____

"A LOT OF OUR PROBLEMS COULD BE SOLVED IF WE WOULD JUST SIT QUIETLY IN A ROOM AND THINK DEEPLY"

PROBLEM:

SOLUTION:

I WOULD LOSE WEIGHT BUT I HATE LOSING, SO...

LIST YOUR FITNESS AND HEALTH GOALS.

_____

_____

_____

_____

_____

_____

_____

_____

_____

_____

_____

_____

_____

_____

_____

_____

_____

I WOULD LOSE WEIGHT BUT I HATE LOSING, SO...

LIST YOUR FITNESS AND HEALTH GOALS.

SHOPPING IS MY CARDIO
WHEN HAVE YOU FELT AT YOUR RICHEST?

SHOPPING IS MY CARDIO

WHEN HAVE YOU FELT AT YOUR RICHEST?

SELF-LOVE IS A PREREQUISTE
BEFORE LOVING ANOTHER

WHAT PART OF YOURSELF DO YOU GUARD MOST CLOSELY? ARE YOU ABLE TO SHARE IT WITH THE PEOPLE YOU LOVE?

SELF-LOVE IS A PREREQUISTE
BEFORE LOVING ANOTHER

WHAT PART OF YOURSELF DO YOU GUARD MOST CLOSELY?
ARE YOU ABLE TO SHARE IT WITH THE PEOPLE YOU LOVE?

THERE, THEIR, THEY'RE

WHAT ARE THE MOST IMPORTANT LIFE LESSONS YOU HAVE LEARNED?

THERE, THEIR, THEY'RE

WHAT ARE THE MOST IMPORTANT LIFE LESSONS YOU HAVE LEARNED?

YOUR FUTURE SELF
WILL THANK YOU

HOW OFTEN DO YOU EXERCISE? COME UP WITH THREE WAYS
YOU AND YOUR FAMILY CAN GET MORE ACTIVE TOGETHER.

YOUR FUTURE SELF WILL THANK YOU

HOW OFTEN DO YOU EXERCISE? COME UP WITH THREE WAYS YOU AND YOUR FAMILY CAN GET MORE ACTIVE TOGETHER.

SOME PEOPLE ARE SO POOR THAT ALL THEY HAVE IS MONEY

IMAGINE YOU HAD $5,000 BUT YOU COULDN'T KEEP IT. YOU HAD TO GIVE IT AWAY TO A PERSON OR CHARITY. WHO WOULD YOU GIVE IT TO & WHY?

SOME PEOPLE ARE SO POOR
THAT ALL THEY HAVE IS MONEY

IMAGINE YOU HAD $5,000 BUT YOU COULDN'T KEEP IT.
YOU HAD TO GIVE IT AWAY TO A PERSON OR CHARITY.
WHO WOULD YOU GIVE IT TO & WHY?

FRIENDLY REMINDER: THIS JOURNAL IS FOR YOUR EYES ONLY

WHAT DO YOU LIKE MOST ABOUT YOUR CURRENT PARTNER? LEAST? (IF SINGLE, WHAT DID YOU LIKE MOST ABOUT YOUR EX? LEAST?)

FRIENDLY REMINDER: THIS JOURNAL IS FOR YOUR EYES ONLY

WHAT DO YOU LIKE MOST ABOUT YOUR CURRENT PARTNER? LEAST? (IF SINGLE, WHAT DID YOU LIKE MOST ABOUT YOUR EX? LEAST?)

NEVER JUDGE A BOOK
BY IT'S MOVIE

WHAT ARE SOME OF THE BEST BOOKS
YOU'VE EVER READ OR LISTENED TO?

NEVER JUDGE A BOOK
BY IT'S MOVIE

WHAT ARE SOME OF THE BEST BOOKS
YOU'VE EVER READ OR LISTENED TO?

TRUE FRIENDS DON'T JUDGE EACH OTHER THEY JUDGE OTHER PEOPLE TOGETHER

DO YOU FEEL LIKE YOU HAVE ENOUGH SUPPORT? IF THE ANSWER IS NO, WHAT ARE SOME WAY YOU CAN START BUILDING UP YOUR SUPPORT SYSTEM?

TRUE FRIENDS DON'T JUDGE EACH OTHER THEY JUDGE OTHER PEOPLE TOGETHER

DO YOU FEEL LIKE YOU HAVE ENOUGH SUPPORT?
IF THE ANSWER IS NO, WHAT ARE SOME WAY YOU
CAN START BUILDING UP YOUR SUPPORT SYSTEM?

I'M ALWAYS RICH AT THE DOLLAR STORE

IS THERE A PAST MONEY MISTAKE FOR WHICH I NEED TO FORGIVE MYSELF AND/OR OTHERS?

I'M ALWAYS RICH AT THE DOLLAR STORE

IS THERE A PAST MONEY MISTAKE FOR WHICH I NEED TO FORGIVE MYSELF AND/OR OTHERS?

WORLD'S OKAY-EST FRIEND

WHO ARE SOME OF YOUR FAVORITE PEOPLE & WHY?

WORLD'S OKAY-EST FRIEND

WHO ARE SOME OF YOUR FAVORITE PEOPLE & WHY?

BUCKET LIST

WHAT ARE SOME THINGS YOU'D LIKE
TO ACCOMPLISH BEFORE YOU DIE?

BUCKET LIST

WHAT ARE SOME THINGS YOU'D LIKE TO ACCOMPLISH BEFORE YOU DIE?

1. WAIST CIRCUMFERENCE:

WHAT'S A HEALTHY WAIST CIRCUMFERENCE?:

2. BODY MASS INDEX (BMI):

WHAT'S A HEALTHY BODY MASS INDEX (BMI)?:

3. BLOOD PRESSURE:

WHAT'S A HEALTHY BLOOD PRESSURE TO HAVE?:

4. CHOLESTEROL:

WHAT'S A HEALTHY CHOLESTEROL LEVEL TO HAVE?:

5. BLOOD SUGAR:

WHAT ARE HEALTHY BLOOD SUGAR LEVELS?:

WRITE DOWN YOUR MEASUREMENTS AND
WEIGHT SO YOU CAN COMPARE THEM LATER. DATE:_____

1. WAIST CIRCUMFERENCE:

WHAT'S A HEALTHY WAIST CIRCUMFERENCE?:

2. BODY MASS INDEX (BMI):

WHAT'S A HEALTHY BODY MASS INDEX (BMI)?:

3. BLOOD PRESSURE:

WHAT'S A HEALTHY BLOOD PRESSURE TO HAVE?:

4. CHOLESTEROL:

WHAT'S A HEALTHY CHOLESTEROL LEVEL TO HAVE?:

5. BLOOD SUGAR:

WHAT ARE HEALTHY BLOOD SUGAR LEVELS?:

"WHETHER YOU THINK YOU CAN, OR YOU THINK YOU CAN'T – YOU'RE RIGHT"

WHAT ARE SOME WAYS I CAN EARN MORE MONEY?:

"WHETHER YOU THINK YOU CAN, OR YOU THINK YOU CAN'T – YOU'RE RIGHT"

WHAT ARE SOME WAYS I CAN EARN MORE MONEY?:

ROUND 2?

THE THING THAT I LOVE MOST ABOUT SEX IS:

_____

_____

_____

_____

_____

_____

_____

_____

_____

_____

_____

_____

_____

_____

_____

_____

_____

_____

ROUND 2?

THE THING THAT I LOVE MOST ABOUT SEX IS:

LIVE IN THE MOMENT
REFLECT LATER.

WHAT ARE YOUR TOP 3 BIGGEST REGRETS? HOW CAN YOU
SHARE THIS WITH THE YOUNGER GENERATION TO HELP
THEM NOT MAKE THE SAME MISTAKES

LIVE IN THE MOMENT REFLECT LATER.

WHAT ARE YOUR TOP 3 BIGGEST REGRETS? HOW CAN YOU SHARE THIS WITH THE YOUNGER GENERATION TO HELP THEM NOT MAKE THE SAME MISTAKES

EXERCISE? THOUGHT YOU SAID EXTRA FRIES

WHAT IS YOUR EXERCISE COMMITMENT?
HOW WILL YOU KEEP IT?

EXERCISE? THOUGHT YOU SAID EXTRA FRIES

WHAT IS YOUR EXERCISE COMMITMENT?
HOW WILL YOU KEEP IT?

DECLARING THE END FROM THE BEGINNING

WHAT DO YOU REALLY WANT?

_____

_____

_____

_____

_____

_____

_____

_____

_____

_____

_____

_____

_____

_____

_____

_____

_____

DECLARING THE END FROM THE BEGINNING

WHAT DO YOU REALLY WANT?

KEEP YOUR EYES ON THE STARS
& YOUR FEET ON THE GROUND

WHAT DO YOU LOVE ABOUT LIFE?

KEEP YOUR EYES ON THE STARS & YOUR FEET ON THE GROUND

WHAT DO YOU LOVE ABOUT LIFE?

TO MOVE FORWARD, SOMETIMES WE NEED TO GO BACK

WHAT ARE SOME OF YOUR FAVORITE CHILDHOOD MEMORIES? WHAT WAS YOUR FAVORITE TOY? CEREAL? GAME?

_____

_____

_____

_____

_____

_____

_____

_____

_____

_____

_____

_____

_____

_____

_____

_____

_____

_____

_____

TO MOVE FORWARD, SOMETIMES
WE NEED TO GO BACK

WHAT ARE SOME OF YOUR FAVORITE CHILDHOOD MEMORIES?
WHAT WAS YOUR FAVORITE TOY? CEREAL? GAME?

Email me at: 25@rahsaanboone.com
and let me know which journal prompt
was most helpful.

Thank you.

RahsaanBoone.com

@25_steps

Made in the USA
Monee, IL
21 February 2021

61018564R10101